W9-AZB-174

Connecticut

A Buddy Book
by
Julie Murray

ABDO
Publishing Company

VISIT US AT
www.abdopub.com

Published by ABDO Publishing Company, 4940 Viking Drive, Edina, Minnesota 55435.

Printed in the United States.

Edited by: Sarah Tieck
Contributing Editor: Michael P. Goecke
Graphic Design: Deb Coldiron, Maria Hosley
Image Research: Sarah Tieck
Photographs: clipart.com, Corbis, Corel, Flat Earth, Getty Images, Library of Congress, North Wind Picture Archives, One Mile Up, PhotoDisc, Photos.com

Library of Congress Cataloging-in-Publication Data

Murray, Julie, 1969-
    Connecticut / Julie Murray.
        p. cm. — (The United States)
    Includes bibliographical references and index.
    ISBN 1-59197-666-9
        1. Connecticut—Juvenile literature. I. Title.

F94.3.M87 2005
974.6—dc22

2004047472

Table Of Contents

A Snapshot Of Connecticut

Connecticut is known for its history and its different types of land. The name Connecticut comes from an Algonquian Indian word. This word meant "on the long tidal river." This name refers to the Connecticut River.

The Connecticut River runs through the middle of Connecticut. Green hills and valleys with rich soil run on both sides of the river. A lot of farmland is found here.

There are 50 states in the United States. Every state is different. Every state has an official state nickname. Connecticut's nickname is the "Constitution State." This is because of Connecticut's history.

The Connecticut River stretches 407 miles (655 km).

Connecticut was one of the first states in the United States. This state fought for freedom from England. People from Connecticut also signed the Declaration of Independence. Connecticut became the fifth state on January 9, 1788.

Connecticut is one of the smallest states in the country. It only covers 5,006 square miles (12,965 sq km) of land. Only Rhode Island and Delaware are smaller.

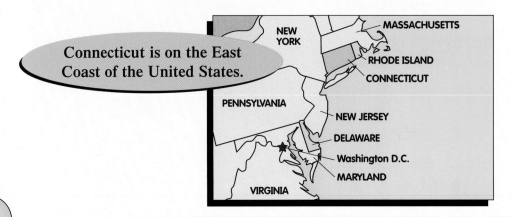

Connecticut is on the East Coast of the United States.

NEW YORK

MASSACHUSETTS

RHODE ISLAND

CONNECTICUT

PENNSYLVANIA

NEW JERSEY

DELAWARE

Washington D.C.

MARYLAND

VIRGINIA

Where Is Connecticut?

There are four parts of the United States. Each part is called a region. Each region is in a different area of the country. The United States Census Bureau says the four regions are the Northeast, the South, the Midwest, and the West.

The state of Connecticut is located in the Northeast region of the United States. The weather in Connecticut changes with each season. Sometimes it is cold and sometimes it is warm.

Four Regions of the United States of America

ALASKA

WASHINGTON

MONTANA

NORTH DAKOTA

MINNESOTA

VERMONT

MAINE

OREGON

IDAHO

SOUTH DAKOTA

WISCONSIN

MICHIGAN

NEW YORK

NEW HAMPSHIRE

MASSACHUSETTS

WYOMING

IOWA

PENNSYLVANIA

RHODE ISLAND

CONNECTICUT

NEVADA

NEBRASKA

ILLINOIS

INDIANA

OHIO

NEW JERSEY

DELAWARE

UTAH

COLORADO

KANSAS

MISSOURI

WEST VIRGINIA

VIRGINIA

Washington D.C.

MARYLAND

CALIFORNIA

KENTUCKY

NORTH CAROLINA

ARIZONA

NEW MEXICO

OKLAHOMA

ARKANSAS

TENNESSEE

SOUTH CAROLINA

MISSISSIPPI

ALABAMA

GEORGIA

TEXAS

LOUISIANA

FLORIDA

HAWAII

West

Midwest

South

Northeast

Connecticut is bordered by New York to the west and Massachusetts to the north. Rhode Island lies to the east. The southern edge of the state runs along Long Island Sound. This is an inlet of the Atlantic Ocean. Sandy beaches and rocky shores line the coast.

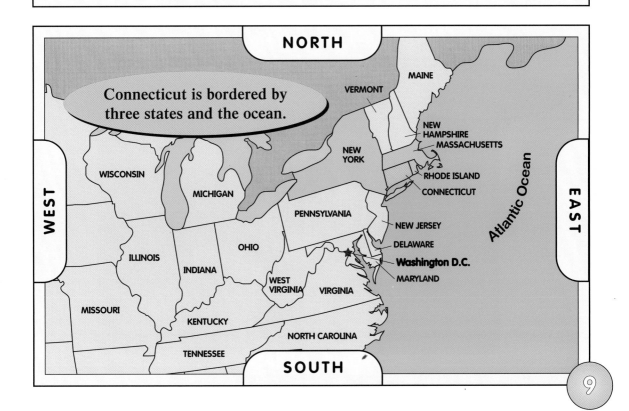

Connecticut is bordered by three states and the ocean.

Connecticut

State abbreviation: CT

State nickname: The Constitution State

State capital: Hartford

State motto: Qui transtulit sustinet (Latin for "He who transplanted still sustains")

Statehood: January 9, 1788, fifth state

Population: 3,405,565, ranks 29th

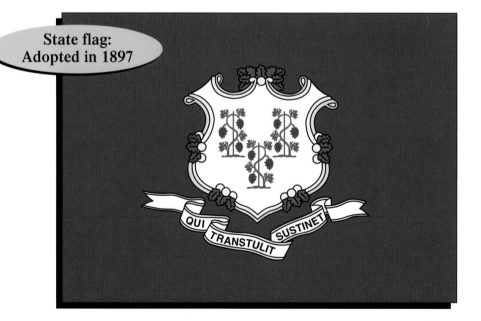

State flag:
Adopted in 1897

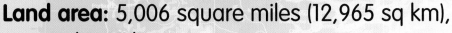

Land area: 5,006 square miles (12,965 sq km), ranks 48th

State tree: White oak

State song: "Yankee Doodle"

State government: Three branches: legislative, executive, and judicial

Average July temperature:
71°F (22°C)

Average January temperature:
26°F (-3°C)

State flower:
Mountain Laurel

State bird:
Robin

State animal:
Sperm Whale

Cities And The Capital

Hartford is the capital of Connecticut. It is the third-largest city in the state. Hartford has many manufacturers. Manufacturers make parts and products. Hartford is sometimes called the "Insurance City." This is because Connecticut is where people first sold insurance. Today, many insurance companies are located there.

The capitol building is in Hartford.

The skyline of Hartford.

Dinosaur State Park is also located near Hartford. At this park, people can see 200 million-year-old dinosaur tracks.

This dinosaur print has become a fossil.

Bridgeport is the largest city in Connecticut. Some people call it the "Park City." This is because the city has many parks. A man named P.T. Barnum helped create those parks for Bridgeport. He was famous for creating the Barnum and Bailey Circus.

People still go to circus performances.

P.T. Barnum

New Haven is Connecticut's second-largest city. It is home to Yale University.

Famous Citizens

Nathan Hale (1755-1776)

Nathan Hale was born in Coventry. He was an American soldier during the Revolutionary War. What made Nathan Hale famous was that he died for helping the United States army. People remember him for saying, "I only regret that I have but one life to lose for my country." This meant he was a hero.

Nathan Hale

Famous Citizens

Katherine Hepburn (1907–2003)

Katherine Hepburn was born in Hartford. She was a famous actress for many years. She was known for movies such as *The African Queen, Little Women,* and *On Golden Pond*. She won four Academy Awards.

Katherine Hepburn

New London Naval Submarine Base

The New London Naval Submarine Base is located in Groton. This is the training center for the United States Navy's submarine fleet. The base opened in 1916.

The USS *Nautilus* was the first nuclear submarine. It was built and launched in Groton in 1954. The USS *Nautilus* is no longer in service. Today, It is called the USS *Nautilus* Memorial.

Crew members stand on top of the USS *Nautilus*.

Yale University

Yale University is located in New Haven. It was founded in 1701. It is the third-oldest institution of higher learning in the United States. Only Harvard University in Massachusetts and the College of William and Mary in Virginia are older.

Yale University is very old. This image of Yale dates back to 1832.

Many famous people studied at Yale. Some Yale graduates were United States presidents. The famous Peabody Museum of Natural History is at Yale University. It is known for its fossil exhibits.

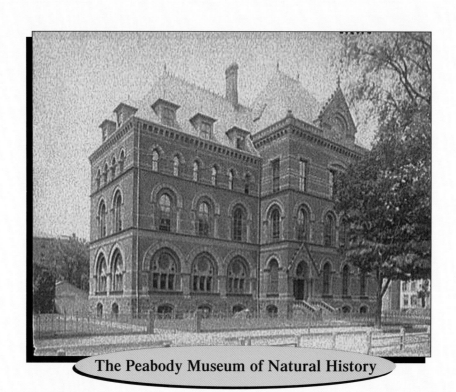

The Peabody Museum of Natural History

Mystic Seaport

Many people visit Mystic Seaport. Mystic Seaport has been rebuilt to look like a whaling village from the 1800s. It is located in the southeastern coastal town of Mystic.

At Mystic Seaport, visitors see an 1800s whaling village come to life.

Mystic Seaport has cobblestone streets. Also, there are many historic buildings from the 1800s. You can see houses, shops, and a school.

There are cobblestone streets in Mystic Seaport.

There are also more than 200 old boats to see. A wooden whaling ship floats in Mystic Seaport. It is called the *Charles W. Morgan*. This is the last American wooden whale ship.

Flags fly from the *Charles W. Morgan*.

Connecticut

1614: Adriaen Block arrives in Connecticut. He claims it for the Dutch.

1633: The first English settlement is in Windsor.

1674: England rules Connecticut.

1701: New Haven and Hartford are both capitals.

1764: The *Hartford Courant* begins publication.

1775: People from Connecticut fight in the Revolutionary War.

1776: Connecticut, along with the other colonies, signs the Declaration of Independence.

1788: Connecticut becomes the fifth state on January 9.

1796: Amelia Simmons publishes *American Cookery*. This was the first cookbook written by an American.

1864: The first accident insurance policy sold in the United States is sold in Hartford. James Goodwin Batterson sold the insurance to James Bolter.

The Declaration of Independence is on display in Washington, D.C.

1875: Hartford is named the capital of Connecticut.

1910: The United States Coast Guard Academy moves to New London.

1954: The USS *Nautilus* is launched at Groton. It was the first nuclear submarine.

1988: Connecticut celebrates 200 years as a state.

Cities in Connecticut

Windsor

Torrington

★ Hartford

Waterbury

Meriden

Norwich

Danbury

New Haven

New London

Mystic

Bridgeport

Groton

Norwalk

Stamford

Important Words

capital a city where government leaders meet.

Declaration of Independence a very important paper of American history. It explains that America is ready to rule itself as an independent country.

fleet a group of ships.

fossil the hardened remains of animals preserved in the earth.

inlet a narrow strip of water flowing to a larger body of water.

insurance a paper that says people are protected against a loss of money if something happens.

nickname a name that describes something special about a person or a place.

nuclear a type of energy that uses atoms.

Web Sites

To learn more about Connecticut, visit ABDO Publishing Company on the World Wide Web. Web site links about Connecticut are featured on our Book Links page. These links are routinely monitored and updated to provide the most current information available.

www.abdopub.com

Index